LIZ CURTIS HIGGS

BAD GIRLS OF THE BIBLE

WORKBOOK

WATERBROOK
PRESS

BAD GIRLS OF THE BIBLE WORKBOOK
PUBLISHED BY WATERBROOK PRESS
2375 Telstar Drive, Suite 160
Colorado Springs, Colorado 80920
A division of Random House, Inc.

All Scripture quotations, unless otherwise indicated, are taken from the *Holy Bible, New International Version*®. NIV®. Copyright © 1973, 1978, 1984 by International Bible Society. Used by permission of Zondervan Publishing House. All rights reserved. Scripture quotations marked (NLT) are taken from the *Holy Bible, New Living Translation,* copyright © 1996. Used by permission of Tyndale House Publishers, Inc., Wheaton, Illinois 60189. All rights reserved. Scripture quotations marked (CEV) are from the *Contemporary English Version.* Copyright © 1991, 1992, 1995 by American Bible Society. Used by permission. Scripture quotations marked (NEB) are from *The New English Bible.* Copyright © 1961, 1970 by the Delegates of the Oxford University Press and the Syndics of the Cambridge University Press.

ISBN 1-57856-545-6

Printed in the United States of America
2005

20 19 18 17 16 15 14 13 12

Contents

YOU GOT IT, SISTER!

Whether you're a Former Bad Girl like me, or an Always Good Girl, I'm glad you're here.

Hundreds of enthusiastic letters and e-mails affirm that God is using *Bad Girls of the Bible* to draw women closer to him—what an answer to prayer! *Bad Girls* Bible studies and reading groups have sprouted up all over the world like colorful wildflowers. Women who know Christ and others willing to explore that sacred relationship have come to learn more about these ancient sisters in Scripture. Wrapped in everything from filmy veils to leopard-print dresses, creative teachers have brought the pages of *Bad Girls of the Bible* to life in urban church basements and rural living rooms, in Sunday school classes and suburban retreat settings.

Talk about changing lives!

Now it's your turn to see what God has in store for you. Maybe you've already read *Bad Girls of the Bible* and are now ready to dive into a deeper study of those wild women…and a deeper understanding of yourself and your relationship with God. Good for you, sis! I wrote this workbook especially for you and for your quiet times with God.

Or perhaps you plan on getting together with a whole group of women to study *Bad Girls of the Bible,* chapter by chapter, and these are the questions you'll be preparing for each week's gathering. Wonderful! Through the pages of this workbook, I'll be right there with you, encouraging us all to grow in grace.

Along with this personal workbook, you'll need: (1) your own copy of the original book, *Bad Girls of the Bible,* (2) your favorite Bible (any translation is fine—I used the *New International Version*), and (3) your favorite pen. (No need for an eraser—there are few "wrong" answers, and besides, it's all about *grace*.)

Before you launch into each lesson in this workbook, I'd recommend reading the entire corresponding chapter in the book, *Bad Girls of the Bible*. The contemporary fiction helps us identify with these women; the verse-by-verse commentary breaks down their biblical stories into manageable bites. The questions provided at the end of each chapter of the main book are included—and greatly expanded and improved—in this workbook, with space for writing answers, making notes, or jotting down comments from others. Go with whatever suits your learning style.

Rather than hurrying through all the questions in the workbook in one sitting, why not take one question per day and savor the lessons God wants to reveal to you? Whenever you have one of those "aha" moments, jot down that realization under Question 8, which is always, "What's the most important lesson you learned…?"

Above all, bring an expectant heart and a prayerful spirit because the Word of God is powerful, dear one, and *you* are about to be changed…for good!

"I am a member of a women's Bible study group named 'The Bad Girls!' Your books have brought together fif-teen women ranging in age from fifteen to eighty. It has become the highlight of my week to meet, pray, study, laugh, and fellowship with this group. We wanted to let you know how much we appreciate your sense of soul and spirit."

Joyce from Alabama

ONE

ALL ABOUT EVIE

Eve

Mrs. Eve, what *were* you thinking? She was thinking she could get away with one little bite, a temptation we understand only too well. Come learn from Eve's mistakes (while we admit a few of our own) and discover how to "Just Say No" when the Enemy says "Go!"

1a. Read **Genesis 3:1-5.** Eve's first two mistakes involved getting into a discussion with the serpent about what God had and had not said, then adding to God's commandment about not eating from that particular tree. Have you ever walked into that kind of trap, either doubting God's Word in your own heart or feeling ill-equipped when you're face to face with someone else who does? Describe the situation.

   b. Did it have the outcome you hoped for? What did you learn from the experience?

c. What do the following verses tell us about God's Word and how we should handle it?

Proverbs 30:5-6

Luke 11:28

2 Timothy 3:16-17

d. What might you do the next time you find yourself getting tangled up in a discussion regarding God's Word?

God was looking not for a good fit but rather a perfect fit.

Liz Curtis Higgs in *Bad Girls of the Bible*, page 23

2a. Read **Genesis 3:5-6.** Eve's next two mistakes weren't oral but visual. She was looking in the wrong place; her eyes were on herself instead of God. And she wanted her eyes to be opened so that she could see everything for herself instead of seeing life through God's eyes. Have you ever gone exploring with your eyes wide open and discovered more than you bargained for?

b. Read our fictional Evie's temptation scene on pages 14-18 in *Bad Girls of the Bible*. List the many mistakes and rationalizations that ultimately led her to violate her father's clear commandment.

c. According to **Proverbs 17:24,** how do our eyes draw us into temptation?

d. To discover for yourself some practical methods we can use to keep our eyes on God, rewrite each verse below in your own words, beginning each statement with, "I will…"

Psalm 119:10

Hebrews 10:25

2 Timothy 2:22

2 Timothy 2:23

Colossians 3:2

Colossians 3:5

Colossians 3:8

e. Underline one of the above statements that are you ready to put into action today. List one specific way you will do so.

When the devil comes a-tempting, he seldom goes in for group conversions.   Liz Curtis Higgs in *Bad Girls of the Bible*, page 26

3a. Read **Genesis 3:5** again. Eve wanted to be like God, knowing good and evil. "I can do it myself" and "I know best" often spill out of our minds if not our mouths. How do the following verses emphasize why being like—that is, equal to—God is impossible?

Isaiah 40:25-26

Isaiah 55:8-9

1 Corinthians 1:25

b. The Lord has made it clear that he has no equal and no one shares his lofty thoughts, yet we're all guilty of wanting to "play God" from time to time. Do you ever find yourself saying, "Why can't everybody do things the right way—my way?" Perhaps being privy to "insider information" is your weakness, giving you a (false) sense of controlling others. How do you connect with Eve on this desire of hers to be "like God"?

c. What practical step might you take to address that all-too-common desire to be in control?

> The wise woman turns her back at the opening hiss and heads for the hills.   Liz Curtis Higgs in *Bad Girls of the Bible*, page 27

4a. Unfortunately, equality with God is exactly what our girl in the garden was hoping to achieve. Read **Genesis 3:6** again. Eve couldn't stop looking at the tree or listening to her growling stomach or marveling at how pretty the fruit was or thinking how helpful it would be to have more knowledge. Our craving for *more* is manifested in every area of our lives. What do you want more of right now…

physically?

emotionally?

spiritually?

b. Do any of those desires dovetail with the Word and will of God? If so, which ones?

c. If not, how can you adjust them to be Christ-centered rather than me-centered?

d. What do the following verses teach us about keeping our lives Christ-centered?

Psalm 73:25-26

Romans 8:5

Romans 13:14

e. What can you suggest as a practical way to begin each day focused on Christ rather than on yourself?

Pleasing to the eye isn't the same as pleasing to God.

Liz Curtis Higgs in *Bad Girls of the Bible*, page 30

5a. Read **Genesis 3:6** once more. (Last time, I promise!) At the very point where Eve could have stopped herself, she didn't. Been there? How do you feel when you don't stop?

b. And how do you feel when you *do* manage to control that urge to sin?

c. What have you learned from those encounters?

d. Eve *did* eat the fruit. What might you have said to her just before the first bite?

e. What does **2 Timothy 1:7** tell us?

f. What might you have said to Eve *after* that fatal bite?

g. What does **James 5:16** tell us to do?

h. But Eve did not confess her sin to her husband. Instead she offered Adam a taste and sinned again. **Proverbs 10:17** tells us what happens when we break the rules. In your own life, who might be "led astray" by your willful actions?

Sin had repercussions, and separation from God was the worst of all.   Liz Curtis Higgs in *Bad Girls of the Bible*, page 34

6a. Eve's big cover-up came next in **Genesis 3:7-8,** where we find her hiding behind skimpy leaves, then hiding behind trees. Can you think of a time you physically tried to cover up the evidence of your sin? Was it effective? Why or why not?

b. Denial is another form of trying to hide our sins, even from ourselves. Is denying or covering up as "serious" a sin as the initial act of disobedience? What does **Isaiah 29:15-16** suggest?

c. Read **Psalm 69:5.** What does this verse remind us about trying to hide our sin?

d. What does **Psalm 32:5** teach us that we should do?

Satan may be cunning, crafty, and clever, but he is in no way equal with God.   Liz Curtis Higgs in *Bad Girls of the Bible*, page 36

7a. Eve's final mistake was one we all make: putting the blame on someone else. Read **Genesis 3:13.** Who did Eve say was responsible?

b. Who or what do you tend to blame first when you sin: a friend? your parents? your husband or children? your job situation? your circumstances? your finances? the Adversary? the Lord?

c. Read **1 John 1:8-9.** How can we stop playing the blame game?

d. **Psalm 51** gives us a biblical model for handling sin in our lives, step by step. According to the following verses, what does David ask God to do for him?

Psalm 51:1

Psalm 51:2

Psalm 51:7

Psalm 51:10

Psalm 51:12

Psalm 51:15

We have no one to blame but ourselves when we choose to sin.
And no one to thank but our Creator when he chooses to
save us from our sins…again.

Liz Curtis Higgs in *Bad Girls of the Bible*, page 39

8. What's the most important lesson you learned from the story of this mother of all Bad Girls, Eve?

Two

BORED TO DISTRACTION

Potiphar's Wife

The tawdry story of Mrs. P demonstrates what can happen when we have too much time on our hands—and not enough attention from loved ones. Boredom, restlessness, self-pity, anger, even loneliness can lead to trouble with a capital *T*. Let's find out what *not* to do from this Egyptian temptress.

1a. Read **Genesis 39:5-7.** Who are the male characters in this biblical story?

b. And how is the woman identified?

c. Why do you think her name is not included in this story?

d. Read **Isaiah 43:1.** Did God know the name given to Potiphar's wife?

e. How do you feel when people refer to you as "the wife of," "the daughter of," "the secretary of," or "the mother of," rather than calling you by your name?

f. Is there a tactful way to share a wider view of your identity, for their sake and your own? What identity is *most* important to you and why?

g. Read **John 15:15.** What does Jesus call you?

h. How might that comfort you when others forget your name?

Everyone knew Potiphar. No one cared enough to remember his wife's name.   Liz Curtis Higgs in *Bad Girls of the Bible,* page 47

2a. Read **1 Corinthians 12:4-5.** What are some ways you can take pride in your various roles, gifts, or areas of service without letting them become a wall you hide behind or a prideful banner you wave above you?

b. Read **1 Corinthians 7:20-21.** God clearly used Joseph right where he was—as a slave. How might God use you right where you are—as the "wife of/mother of/employee of" someone more prominent than you are?

c. Whatever your role(s), what advice does the apostle Paul offer in **Ephesians 4:1-2?**

d. Which one of those qualities do you need to develop most in your life right now?

> Hers was a sin of commission; her husband's, one of omission.
>
> Liz Curtis Higgs in *Bad Girls of the Bible*, page 52

3a. Joseph's determination to honor God helped him avoid the wicked ways of Potiphar's wife, aptly described in **Proverbs 2:16-19.** What do those verses tell us about an adulteress? Specifically…

How does she entice men?

What vows does she break?

Where will such an affair lead?

b. Read **Genesis 39:7-10.** The story of the scorned adulteress is a common one in movies and literature. What examples, from the silver screen *or* from real life, might you give?

c. Do such stories—fictional or factual—ever have a happy ending?

d. Read **Exodus 20:14.** What is God's clear commandment concerning adultery?

e. What are some of the justifications—let's be blunt: *excuses*—people give for having an affair?

f. **Ephesians 4:18-19** describes the oversexed nature of life in the first century—and the twenty-first century—perfectly. What do those verses reveal about how our hearts become hardened against sexual purity?

g. Read **Proverbs 6:32-34.** List all the possible repercussions, for the husband or the wife, of breaking one's marriage vows.

Unlike Joseph's coat of many colors, hers came in one shade: solid black.   Liz Curtis Higgs in *Bad Girls of the Bible*, page 53

4a. Read **Genesis 39:6.** Was Potiphar at all to blame for his wife's wandering eye? If so, how did he fail her?

b. According to the following verses, what does God expect from husbands?

Proverbs 5:18

Malachi 2:15

Ephesians 5:25-28

c. And what is the wife's responsibility, according to **Ephesians 5:22-25**?

d. What do you think Mrs. P might have done to honor her husband and her marriage vows…and garner his attention?

e. If you're married, does your husband ever behave like Potiphar, giving priority to work or other interests rather than to his relationship with you? If so, how might you get his attention (short of a tossing a frying pan across his forehead!) and draw his affection back to you?

f. How might a married woman make the same mistake, ignoring her husband and unintentionally pushing him into another woman's arms?

g. **Proverbs 20:6** suggests that faithful men are few and far between. But that doesn't mean we are blameless if a married man looks our way. If you're single, how can you avoid "catching" the eye of such a man and convincing yourself that if his wife can't make him happy, you can?

> She accused the innocent Joseph of the very behavior of
> which she herself was guilty.
>
> Liz Curtis Higgs in *Bad Girls of the Bible*, page 55

5a. Read **Genesis 39:7** again. What do you think she was doing for "a while" before she propositioned Joseph?

b. It's obvious what Mrs. P had on her mind. How can we fill our idle time (if we have any!) with appropriate thoughts?

c. Some women remain physically pure yet indulge in a romantic, even sexually explicit fantasy life. What does Jesus tell us in **Matthew 5:27-28**?

d. How can we keep our minds and imaginations from going places we know aren't pleasing to God?

e. Read **1 Thessalonians 4:3-7** and **Colossians 3:5.** Are there specific things you need to avoid, such as R-rated movies? Internet temptations? steamy novels? List them here, underlining those things in your home that it's time to do away with, right now.

f. **Philippians 4:8** encourages us to replace those things that are unholy with things that are good. What sort of positive additions might you make in your life to purify your thoughts and therefore your actions?

g. Read the fictional story from the bottom of page 45 to the top of page 46, then read **Genesis 39:8-9.** In both stories, whom does Joseph say he will dishonor if he sleeps with her?

And why is that true?

h. Read **Genesis 39:10.** In what ways did Joseph resist her advances?

i. What does that teach us about avoiding temptation?

One smooth lie always begets another.

Liz Curtis Higgs in *Bad Girls of the Bible*, page 55

6a. Joseph did the right thing and ran. Mrs. Potiphar did the wrong thing—again, still—and ran her mouth. Read **Genesis 39:13-15.** To whom did she lie first?

b. Read **Genesis 39:16.** Why do you think she kept his cloak handy?

c. Mrs. P repeated her false accusation in **Genesis 39:17-18.** To whom was she speaking?

d. How is this statement about Joseph's supposed indiscretion different than the one a few verses earlier?

e. What does this reveal about Mrs. P's motivations?

f. What steps—if any—might Joseph, the godly man in both the fictional and biblical stories, have taken to avoid the revenge-filled conclusion?

g. Even though we can't always control the outcome when we are falsely accused, what can we control?

h. The biblical Joseph landed in jail, yet remained close to God, who used him mightily. In what ways does **Psalm 15:1-5** reflect Joseph's life?

i. How should a godly person handle unfair and false accusations?

j. According to **Proverbs 2:7-8,** what will God do for us if we are blameless?

k. List the ways Joseph's jail sentence resulted in protection rather than punishment.

l. Can you describe a time you felt punished and then later realized you had been protected?

m. What comfort can we draw from **Psalm 37:18**?

We never know when temptation will arrive at our doorsteps.

Liz Curtis Higgs in *Bad Girls of the Bible*, page 56

7a. I chose the name "Mitzi" for Mrs. P's fictional counterpart because it comes from a Hebrew word meaning "small or bitter." Though her obvious sin was lust, perhaps the root of her sin was bitterness and anger at being ignored by Potiphar and rejected by this Hebrew slave. Do anger or bitterness ever rear their ugly heads in your own life? If so, what situations are most likely to trigger those emotions?

b. Read **Genesis 39:19.** Her anger triggered someone else's wrath...whose?

c. What do the following verses tell us about anger and where it leads?

James 1:19-20

Psalm 37:8

d. **Colossians 3:8** includes a list of sins that stem from anger. Jot them down here.

e. If "filthy language" is an area you struggle with in your life, how could you put on the brakes?

f. Write out **Ephesians 4:26-27** on a three-by-five-inch index card. Where might you post it to the best advantage?

The snazziest lipstick in the world can't compete with clean lips ...and a clean heart.   Liz Curtis Higgs in *Bad Girls of the Bible*, page 57

8. What's the most important lesson you've learned from the tragic, timeless story of Potiphar's wife?

THREE

PILLAR OF THE COMMUNITY

Lot's Wife

Fewer phrases are sadder than the ones that begin, "If only…" For those of us with a multitude of regrets for past failures, the story of Lot's wife is a sobering reminder that a day of judgment is on our horizon. Here's the good news: There's still time to change our direction and walk in grace!

1a. We never hear a word from Mrs. Lot's own lips. Do you know women like Lot's wife—exceedingly quiet, willing to let their husbands do all the talking and make the important decisions?

b. According to **Proverbs 17:1** and **1 Peter 3:1-6,** what are some of the advantages of wifely reticence?

c. And what are the dangers, if any, of being a silent partner in a marriage relationship?

d. Where do you fall on the scale of quiet to noisy?

e. What do the following verses teach us about how God can work in the quiet moments of our lives?

Job 6:24

Psalm 23:2-3

Zephaniah 3:17

f. If Lot's wife had been wise enough to do as King David did in **Psalm 39:2-4** and end her apparent silence, what might the Lord's response have been to her?

g. Knowing how brief our lives are, is there anything you need to "speak up" and tell the Lord about today?

No one is ever prepared for disaster to strike.

Liz Curtis Higgs in *Bad Girls of the Bible*, page 66

2a. **Genesis 18:23-33** describes Abraham asking God to be merciful to the few good souls in Sodom and Gomorrah. What does this conversation tell you about Abraham?

b. And what does it reveal about God?

c. Was there a time you interceded for your family in this way, asking God for mercy?

d. Read **2 Peter 2:4-9.** Why did God spare Lot and his family?

e. Lot dragged his feet the entire journey. How can you explain God's patience with Lot? See **Nehemiah 9:31.**

f. Do you try God's patience at times? Think of an example from the last week or so.

g. Read **2 Peter 3:9.** What is God patiently waiting for you to do?

h. If you were to "get what you deserve" from God, what would that be? See **Romans 6:23.**

i. In **1 Timothy 1:16** we learn why the gift of grace is extended to us. Rewrite that powerful verse in your own words, applying it to your own faith journey.

God's mercy stretches further than we can imagine.
Liz Curtis Higgs in *Bad Girls of the Bible*, page 67

3a. Read **Genesis 19:1-3.** How does **Hebrews 13:2** relate to Lot's treatment of the two mysterious men at the city gate?

b. **Genesis 19:4-7** gives us a disgustingly accurate picture of why God wanted to destroy Sodom and Gomorrah. How do you think Lot managed to be different from all those wicked men?

c. Now read **Genesis 19:8.** How do you handle a scene like that? Turn away from it? Pretend it isn't in the Bible? Hide it from your children? Get angry about it? Why do you think this particular part of the story is included in Scripture? What could we possibly learn from it?

d. Do you think this sort of tragedy occurred only in ancient times, or do we see similar events happening around the world today with parents "sacrificing" their children on the altar of self-preservation?

e. Closer to home—and on a much milder scale—can you think of a time you reacted poorly in a panicky situation involving your children?

f. **Nehemiah 4:14** declares that we are to defend our loved ones. According to the following verses, how does God stand with parents in protecting their children?

Proverbs 14:26

2 Corinthians 6:18

What's a sofa compared to survival?

Liz Curtis Higgs in *Bad Girls of the Bible*, page 74

4a. Read **Genesis 19:12-14.** Lot's sons-in-law thought he was joking. Why wouldn't they have taken him seriously?

b. Read **Psalm 123:3-4.** If you've ever warned someone about a potential disaster and had him or her laugh at your fears, how did that make you feel?

c. We all have people in our lives who are headed for eternal punishment as outlined in **2 Thessalonians 1:8-9.** For what will they be punished?

d. And what will their punishment entail?

e. Who in your life needs to be warned?

f. What will it take for you to risk being laughed at—or scoffed or ridiculed—in order to communicate the truth?

g. What does **Luke 6:22-23** tell us to do when we are scorned for sharing our faith?

h. In **1 Thessalonians 4:8,** we learn that they are *not* rejecting us. Who, then?

i. The following verses are meant to encourage you. Note how they do so.

1 Corinthians 15:57-58

Ephesians 6:7-8

Colossians 3:23-24

Grace at work once more—and they fought it tooth and nail.

Liz Curtis Higgs in *Bad Girls of the Bible*, page 74

5a. Even with salvation from certain death assured them, Lot and his family tarried. Read page 74 of *Bad Girls of the Bible*. Why do *you* think they're stalling?

b. Read **Genesis 19:17.** Has the Lord ever given you directives as clearly as the angels did to Mrs. Lot—"Don't look!" or "Don't stop!"? If so, jot down what you sensed God told you specifically *not* to do.

And what was the outcome?

c. **Hebrews 12:10-11** explains why God disciplines us with "dos" and "don'ts." Is discipline meant to be an enjoyable process? Why or why not?

d. What are the fruits of our obedience?

e. Which command is harder for you to obey—a "don't" or a "do"? Why?

f. What do the following verses tell us *not* to do?

Matthew 6:19

Matthew 6:25

Matthew 6:34

g. In light of those "do nots," read pages 60-61 in *Bad Girls of the Bible.* What can you find our fictional Lottie doing that the Lord told us *not* to do in the verses above?

h. How do you identify with Lottie?

i. What would be the hardest thing for you to walk away from, or release from your grasp?

j. If God asked you to do so—right now—how could you do it?

k. Read **Matthew 6:20-21.** Where are we to store our treasures?

l. How might we do that?

It was divine judgment, not a geological surprise.

Liz Curtis Higgs in *Bad Girls of the Bible*, page 76

6a. Read **Genesis 19:18-20.** Why did Lot ask to run to Zoar rather than to the mountains?

b. **Genesis 19:21-22** shows us how the angelic man responded. Were you surprised at his willingness to change his plans? Why do you think he agreed?

c. Do you ever bargain with God like that? If so, think of an instance when your request was answered…or when it was not answered.

d. Did that build your faith…or threaten it?

e. What are we to learn from Lot's example of asking for another option?

f. Read **Exodus 4:10-15** to see how Moses bargained with God. What did Moses use as an excuse *not* to do what the Lord asked of him?

g. What was God's initial response?

h. Then what did Moses ask God to do?

i. I've said those very words to God a time or two…have you? In my case, God said, "Go anyway, Liz!" What was the Lord's response to you?

j. Whether we argue with God or go willingly, what is the result—in Lot's situation, in Moses's case, in our own lives?

She was offered salvation yet turned away from it.

Liz Curtis Higgs in *Bad Girls of the Bible*, page 79

7a. In **Genesis 19:23-25** we learn that, indeed, God's will was accomplished. **Genesis 19:26** is our key verse. Write it out here.

b. On pages 77-78 of *Bad Girls of the Bible*, read the list of ten reasons why Lot's wife may have turned back toward Sodom. Which one makes the most sense to you?

c. Do you think she intentionally chose death over life? Why or why not?

d. How might the following verses address Mrs. Lot's dire situation?

Psalm 116:3

Proverbs 13:19

2 Corinthians 7:10

e. Why do you think we aren't told more about Lot's wife in this story and, in particular, about her decision to turn back?

His grace has no limits…except time.

Liz Curtis Higgs in *Bad Girls of the Bible*, page 81

8. What's the most important lesson you've learned from the salty tale of Lot's wife?

FOUR

DYING FOR A DRINK

The Woman at the Well

I see a pattern forming here, don't you? A third Bad Girl without a name. Yet even without a nametag to jog our memories, we'll never forget her story. This woman was bold, brassy, and bent on getting her thirst quenched…and boy, did she ever!

1a. Our Bad Girl is introduced in **John 4:7.** We're told her gender and her nationality, but not told her name. Why might that be?

b. Read **John 10:14.** Did Jesus know her name?

c. According to **Psalm 139:13-16,** how well does God know his created beings?

d. I chose the name "Crystal" for her fictional counterpart because Jesus could see right through her, like crystal clear water. Does the omission of the Samaritan woman's name make her real-life story more *or* less believable to you?

More *or* less powerful? Why?

e. As a woman and a Samaritan, she was probably not educated or strong or famous or rich. What does **Jeremiah 9:23-24** tell us matters most to God?

f. She came looking for water but instead found Jesus. Read **John 4:6-9.** Was their meeting at the well a "coincidence"…or a "God-incidence"? What leads you to this conclusion?

g. What do these verses tell us about the paths our lives take?

Job 31:4

Proverbs 16:9

Jeremiah 10:23

h. How might those verses comfort or encourage you?

Her gender and her nationality are not incidental to the story; they are integral.   Liz Curtis Higgs in *Bad Girls of the Bible*, page 92

2a. **John 4:6** tells us the Samaritan woman went to the well in the heat of the day rather than the cool of the evening. Who or what do you think she was avoiding? Why?

b. Think of a time when you were treated as "less than" by your peers, or felt judged by "religious" people. How did you handle the situation? Confrontation? Avoidance? Begrudging acceptance?

c. How does **1 Peter 2:19** tell us to handle such injustice?

d. Read **Matthew 7:1-2.** What happens to us when we judge other people?

e. **Luke 6:36-37** teaches us what to do instead of judging. Write out verse 36 here.

f. If forgiveness and reconciliation are going to happen, who should reach out first, and why?

g. Read **1 Thessalonians 5:15.** This simple direction is very hard to obey in a payback culture like ours! Where would you get the strength to pay back wrong with right?

h. What might **John 4:10** suggest as our source of strength and refreshment?

An endless supply of holy, cleansing water awaited the Samaritan woman.   Liz Curtis Higgs in *Bad Girls of the Bible*, page 94

3a. Read **John 4:11-15.** The woman at the well was thirstier than she realized What are you "thirsty" for, spiritually?

b. What have you been reaching for (for example, work, hobbies, materialism, busyness) instead of the living water Christ offers?

c. Have any of those things quenched your thirst? Why or why not?

d. The prophet, Amos, recorded God's promise that one day the whole world would be thirsty. What does **Amos 8:11** tell us the world will be thirsty for most?

e. According to **Isaiah 41:17,** who will respond to our thirst?

f. **John 7:37-38** echoes the same theme. What invitation did Jesus offer to those attending the Feast of Tabernacles?

g. God's Word tells us that it's not a shame to be thirsty—it's a blessing! Write out **Matthew 5:6.**

When Christ speaks to my heart, it's always just the two of us.

Liz Curtis Higgs in *Bad Girls of the Bible*, page 93

4a. According to **John 4:7-8,** who spoke first? Why was that necessary?

b. What do you think prompted the Samaritan woman to respond to this stranger?

c. Read **Psalm 138:3.** How can we be certain boldness is a godly attribute?

d. What is the difference between a godly woman boldly reaching beyond her comfort zone and a pushy dame?

e. Read the story of the queen of Sheba in **1 Kings 10:1-13.** Compare the attributes of this bold queen and our bold but nameless woman at the well.

	QUEEN OF SHEBA	WOMAN AT THE WELL
Nationality?		
Social status?		
Payment offered?		
Thirst for truth?		
Thirst quenched?		

f. What might this comparison teach you?

g. According to **Hebrews 10:19-22,** what assurances are we given that allow us to boldly approach God's throne?

h. What "hard question" would you like to boldly ask God right now?

i. How might you go about finding his answer for you?

It's always easier to talk about church than to talk about Christ.   Liz Curtis Higgs in *Bad Girls of the Bible*, page 97

5a. Check out the fascinating shift in conversation in **John 4:16-20.** At what point did our Samaritan sister get uneasy with the direction their discussion was going and abruptly change the subject? Why?

b. The woman at the well had had many husbands, yet the Word tells us that Jesus is our true husband. Read **Ephesians 5:25-27** and **Isaiah 54:4-5.** According to these verses, what can Jesus do for us that no earthly husband could possibly do?

c. Despite her five-husband past and immoral present, Jesus extended living water to this thirsty woman, changing her future forever. Read **Titus 3:3-7.** What truths in this passage give you hope?

Jesus saw past her hardened exterior to the parched interior of her soul.   Liz Curtis Higgs in *Bad Girls of the Bible*, page 98

6a. Read **John 4:27.** When the disciples arrived, why do you suppose they didn't intervene in the conversation?

b. **John 4:31-34** shows that the disciples were every bit as fixated on physical needs as the woman was. She was thinking about water. What were they thinking about?

c. Why do you suppose this sidebar was included in the story? And for whose benefit?

d. In **John 4:35-38** Jesus instructed his disciples about seedtime and harvest in God's kingdom. See if you can draw lines matching the various elements of his teaching with what they might represent:

The reapers	The whole world
The sower	God's Word
The seed	The Disciples
The field	New believers
The harvest	God

How does this lesson connect to the Samaritan woman's story that surrounds it?

Filled with living water, she sought other thirsty souls.

Liz Curtis Higgs in *Bad Girls of the Bible*, page 99

7a. Read **John 4:28.** Why do you think she left behind her water jar?

b. **Matthew 9:17** and **2 Corinthians 5:17** address the difference between our old selves and our new selves in Christ. What might that old water jar represent in the Samaritan woman's life?

c. What old water jar might you need to leave behind before you can share the good news with others?

d. List all the reasons—whether righteous or selfish—you think the Samaritan woman hurried back to the town to tell everyone she'd met the Messiah.

e. If you've shared your faith with people who know you well, hairy past and all, what were your reasons for doing so?

f. In each of the following verses, find the best reasons of all to share the gospel.

Acts 20:24

1 Corinthians 9:22-23

1 Thessalonians 2:8

g. In **John 4:29-30,** the Samaritan woman extended an invitation to her hearers: "Come, see a man…" Why did she not simply say, "Stay put and let me tell you"?

h. Read **John 4:39-42.** What was the outcome of their responding to her invitation to come and see Jesus?

i. Listed near the bottom of page 99 of *Bad Girls of the Bible* are two things that happen when we meet the Christ. Write them here.

(1)

(2)

Which is the hardest for you to do? Why?

A changed life gets people's attention every time.

Liz Curtis Higgs in *Bad Girls of the Bible*, page 100

---

8. What's the most important lesson you've learned from the life-changing story of the unnamed woman at the well?

FIVE

THE FIRST CUT
IS THE DEEPEST

Delilah

O*uch.* Delilah's story slices too close to my silver-lovin' heart. Forced to choose between a mercurial lover and a mercenary dollar…well, I'm not convinced I'd do much better than Miss D did so many centuries ago. Let's see if Delilah's weaknesses (Samson's too) offer a lesson we all need to learn.

1a. What weaknesses do you find in Samson's life as described in the verses listed below?

Judges 15:3

Judges 15:4-5

Judges 15:6-8

Judges 16:1-3

b. Perhaps the underlying problem beneath all of Samson's weaknesses—well, *sins*—was pride. **Proverbs 21:24** describes such a man.
   What do these verses tell us about that most familiar human vice?

   Psalm 10:4

   Psalm 73:6

   Proverbs 16:18

c. What evidence do you see of that same weakness in your own life?

d. Perhaps Samson struggled with pride because he led a uniquely
   blessed life from conception. Jot down the unique aspects of Samson's
   life recorded in these verses.

   Judges 13:2-5

   Judges 13:24-25

   Judges 14:5-6

e. Now read **Judges 16:18-21.** Uh-oh. What happened?

f. Finally, read **Judges 16:28-30.** How did God answer Samson's prayer?

g. The prophet Isaiah's words recorded in **Isaiah 2:11** suit the outcome of this mighty turnabout well. Write the verse out here.

h. In what ways does that verse describe Samson's final act?

For a guy who was supposed to avoid dead bodies, Samson
surely created a ton of them.

Liz Curtis Higgs in *Bad Girls of the Bible*, page 113

2a. Read **Proverbs 7:21-23.** Perhaps the writer of Proverbs was thinking
of someone like Delilah when those verses were first recorded. What
similarities do you find?

b. Now read Delilah's sordid story in **Judges 16:4-20.** According to the
following passages, what weaknesses—yes, *sins*—did Delilah demonstrate?

Judges 16:5-6

Judges 16:9-10

Judges 16:15-16

Judges 16:18

c. What evidence of any of those same sins have you seen in your own life?

d. Perhaps women identify most with the activity described in verse 16—*nagging*. Read again page 119 of *Bad Girls of the Bible*. Is nagging effective—that is, does it produce the results you want? Why or why not?

> Even strong men can harbor a hidden weakness.
>
> Liz Curtis Higgs in *Bad Girls of the Bible*, page 115

3a. As we've already noted in **Judges 15:7,** Samson was often depicted as taking revenge for one wrong or another. Could Delilah have been seeking revenge too—against the Philistines perhaps, or men who had used her in the past? What are some possibilities that might have suited her personality and station in life?

b. Think of an example from your own life when you wanted to hurt someone—physically, emotionally, financially, socially—because he or she hurt you first. Did you take some form of revenge? If so, what was it and what was the result? If not, how were you able to stop the urge to strike back?

c. How does our current entertainment culture—movies, books, television, video games—depict revenge? Is it presented as an honorable or dishonorable motive?

d. Think of a silver-screen example. Was this avenger portrayed as a hero or villain?

e. Read **Leviticus 19:18** in the Old Testament and **Romans 12:19** in the New Testament. According to those verses, has human revenge ever been appropriate? Why or why not?

f. Read **Nahum 1:2-3,** then write down all the adjectives in that passage that describe our holy avenger.

g. In light of that, read **Judges 13:5; 14:4;** and **16:28.** Is it possible God planned to use Samson all along to enact his righteous revenge against the Philistines? What clues do these three verses give you that such might be the case?

h. Samson did not always walk worthy of his godly calling, but the Lord worked through his chosen servant nonetheless. How does that encourage you in your own walk with God?

The operative word for Delilah might be *pawn*.

Liz Curtis Higgs in *Bad Girls of the Bible*, page 115

4a. Consider Delilah's motives for a moment by looking deep inside her heart. What do you see there? An angry woman? A hurt child? A deserted wife? A greedy harlot? Think of all the ways you might describe her, based on the scriptural story and your own experiences as a woman.

b. Though the following words from the prophet Isaiah were spoken to the nation of Israel, note how each of the verses applies to Delilah's story.

Isaiah 30:12

Isaiah 30:13

c. In **Isaiah 30:15,** the prophet suggests a more redemptive solution... *if* we change our behavior. What does the Lord ask us to do?

d. Of the phrases mentioned there, which one might be the hardest for you to do...and why?

e. It all comes down to a matter of trust. What does **Isaiah 26:4** assure us? What do you need to trust God to handle in your life right now?

Delilah didn't feel sorry for him. She felt rich.

Liz Curtis Higgs in *Bad Girls of the Bible*, page 120

5a. Let's "follow the money." How much do you suppose the huge financial reward influenced Delilah's decision to deceive Samson?

b. What additional motivation might have driven her to take scissors in hand?

c. On page 120 of *Bad Girls of the Bible,* a comparison is made between Delilah and Judas. Read the following verses, noting the similarities —and differences—in the stories of these two traitors.

	WHAT JUDAS DID	WHAT DELILAH DID
Matthew 26:14		
Matthew 26:15		
Matthew 26:16		
Mark 14:43		
Mark 14:44		
Mark 14:45		

d. Though both of these greedy people betrayed someone close to them for the sake of silver, God ordained that these deeds would take place for the sake of his kingdom. Read **Judges 16:27-30.** Again, whose will was accomplished?

e. **Matthew 27:3-5** tells us what happened to Judas. Now read the top half of page 123 of *Bad Girls of the Bible.* Do you think Delilah was among those killed when the temple collapsed? Why or why not?

f. It's easy to criticize the mercenary natures of Delilah and Judas from a distance. Now let's look a little closer to home. If you've ever taken a job simply for the money or in any way been influenced by a desire for monetary gain, what did you learn from that experience?

g. Read **Ezekiel 7:19.** Have you ever wanted to give back money that seemed tainted or ill gotten? If so, describe your experience.

h. Are there "Philistines" in your life now, tempting you with easy money?

i. What wisdom does **1 Peter 1:18-19** provide for handling such temptations?

The silver didn't represent Samson's price; it was *her* price.

Liz Curtis Higgs in *Bad Girls of the Bible*, page 121

6a. Why was Samson so easily deceived? Was that Delilah's fault or his?

b. **First Corinthians 3:18** cautions us to be aware of self-deception. Where are the blind spots in your own life where you tend to see only what you want to see? At work? With your children? With certain friends?

c. What do you need to do—practically and specifically—to avoid being ensnared like Samson, who was dragged where he didn't want to go and imprisoned by his enemies?

d. Sometimes we're not blinded by greed like Delilah or just plain blinded like Samson; we're simply looking in the wrong direction. Read **Hebrews 12:1-2** and **Psalm 25:15.** Where should we be looking?

e. What benefit do we receive when we focus our eyes in the right direction?

f. What was the "joy" that Christ fixed his gaze upon?

Even with all his failings, [Samson] still had a heart for God.

Liz Curtis Higgs in *Bad Girls of the Bible*, page 123

7a. Samson's greatest weakness was Delilah...and pride was a close second! When all was said and done (and destroyed), what do you think was Delilah's greatest weakness? Lust? Greed? Idolatry, which includes anything in our lives that gets priority over God? Selfishness? Make a convincing case for one of those possibilities.

"I think Delilah's greatest sin was _____ because

b. How do any of the sins mentioned above rear their ugly heads in your own life?

c. What could you do to surrender that weakness to the lordship of Christ? Here are some verses to encourage you. (Choose the sin that hits closest to home!)

Lust   **1 Thessalonians 4:3-5**

Greed   **Luke 9:25**

Idolatry   **1 Corinthians 10:13-14**

Selfishness   **Philippians 2:3-4**

What Delilah gained in goods she surely lost in relationships.

Liz Curtis Higgs in *Bad Girls of the Bible*, page 124

8. What's the most important lesson you've learned from the dark, disastrous story of Samson and Delilah?

SIX

GENEROUS TO A FAULT

Sapphira

Sapphira was a gem, all right: cool, smooth, and as sharp-edged as the gemstone for which she was named. Was it the color of her eyes or the hardness of her heart, I wonder, that earned her such a lovely name—and first-century shame? All I know is, her story scares me to death! Which, no doubt, is exactly what the Lord intended.

1a. Read **Acts 4:32-35** for an eye-opening look at the early church. How does the idea of believers pooling their resources for the common good strike you? Good idea or bad idea? Why?

b. Describe any instances where you've seen such selfless generosity work in your own corner of the world, maybe between neighbors or within families, if not in whole congregations.

c. What *practical* reasons might you offer for *not* sharing everything with one another in your church family?

d. And what *emotional* reasons might prevent you from sharing your material possessions and financial resources freely with other believers?

e. According to **Luke 12:33-34,** what does Jesus urge his followers to do…and why?

f. What do you treasure most in life?

g. What does that reflect about your heart?

h. Would those who know you best agree with that self-assessment?

i. Read **1 John 3:17-18.** How do these verses describe how true love is expressed?

j. Read **Acts 2:44-45.** How could we as God's church be more loving—specifically, more generous—with one another?

k. What steps do you need to take in your own life to move toward a more generous spirit and loosen your grasp on material things?

At first blush Sapphira was a Good Girl, not a Bad one.

Liz Curtis Higgs in *Bad Girls of the Bible*, page 137

2a. Read **Acts 4:36-37.** Barnabas was doing exactly what other committed believers were doing, according to what we learned earlier in **Acts 4:34-35.** Why do you think he was singled out as the "Son of Encouragement"?

b. Now read **Acts 5:1-2.** What do you think motivated Ananias and Sapphira to give their money to the apostles?

c. Why do you think they kept some for themselves?

d. Did they know that was the wrong thing to do? What leads you to that conclusion?

e. What are some reasons people donate money to a good cause, other than a purely generous spirit? (To get your mental wheels turning, reread page 128 of *Bad Girls of the Bible* and check out the motives behind Sofia's desire to give to the Philanthropic Society!)

f. When your own motives are less than virtuous, what deep emotional need might be the impetus for your giving? Are you a people pleaser? someone who needs applause? desperate to impress others? Do you like to feel superior to those who cannot—or choose not to—be as generous? (Please be totally honest here, sis—this is *your* workbook!)

g. Read **Philippians 3:7-9.** How could the needs of your heart be met in a more godly fashion, rather than through public recognition of giving?

h. The following verses address the virtues of generosity. Note the benefits that are mentioned in each.

Psalm 112:5

Proverbs 11:25

2 Corinthians 9:13

It's clear that the twosome were working in tandem.

Liz Curtis Higgs in *Bad Girls of the Bible*, page 138

3a. Read **Luke 12:15.** Part of Sapphira's problem was a case of "keeping up with the (Barnabas) Joneses." How can we resist that natural-but-not-nice drive to play "me too"—in both what we conspicuously give away *and* what we covertly keep?

b. **Proverbs 23:5** perfectly describes our modern stock market woes! If you've ever lost money—in unexpected taxes, in stock or insurance losses, in an estate settlement, or something similar—how did you first respond?

c. How has your perspective about that experience changed with the passing of time?

d. What practical lesson did you learn in the process?

e. And what *spiritual* lesson did it teach you? (Hint: They often are exactly the same lesson!)

f. Our culture is steeped in materialism—the he-who-dies-with-the-most-stuff-wins mentality. What advice do we find in the following verses about financial resources?

1 Timothy 6:17

1 Timothy 6:18

1 Timothy 6:19

g. That last phrase of verse 19 is translated in several ways:
   • "take hold of the life that is truly life" (NIV)
   • "take hold of real life" (NLT)
   • "know what true life is like" (CEV)
   • "grasp the life which is life indeed" (NEB)
   What does "real life"—Life with a capital *L*—mean to you?

The issue was honesty, not money.

Liz Curtis Higgs in *Bad Girls of the Bible*, page 138

4a. Read **Acts 5:3-4.** What excuses do you suppose Ananias and Sapphira gave each other to justify their subterfuge?

b. The money itself wasn't the problem. Read **Acts 5:3-4** again. What key word appears in both verses, clearly pointing to Ananias's sin?

c. What does **Ephesians 4:25** teach us on that subject?

d. Have you ever planned to give a certain amount to the Lord's work, then changed your mind at the last minute and lowered the dollar figure? Did you have a valid reason…or were you lying to yourself?

e. Read **2 Corinthians 9:6-7.** The next time you reach into your wallet or get out your checkbook during the offertory, what biblical truth do you need to have clearly in mind when you choose how much to give?

Ananias wasn't *mostly* dead. He was history.

Liz Curtis Higgs in *Bad Girls of the Bible*, page 140

5a. If they truly needed the money they held back, what options did Ananias and Sapphira have instead of hiding it?

b. What is the difference between investing money in a portfolio and hoarding it?

c. Does tucking money away indicate prudent planning or a lack of faith?

d. Read the parable of the talents in **Matthew 25:14-30.** (Here, a "talent" means money—about six thousand drachmas, a silver coin of that era.) What did both the man with five talents and the man with two talents do with their money?

e. Compare verse 21 and verse 23. Even though the amounts the men invested—and earned—were different, how are the two rewarded?

f. What does the man with one talent do with his money?

g. According to **Matthew 25:28-30,** how is that man…uh…rewarded?

h. What similarities do you see between the story of Ananias and Sapphira and Jesus' parable of the talents?

They tested God's strength against their own…and lost.

Liz Curtis Higgs in *Bad Girls of the Bible*, page 141

6a. Read page 143 in *Bad Girls of the Bible*. If my story of the price sticker at the airport brought to mind any similar experience of your own, how did you handle it…or *wish* you'd handled it?

b. Why might something seemingly insignificant—three dollars plus tax—be important to God?

c. Read **Jeremiah 17:10.** Does this verse comfort you…or concern you? Why?

d. How does **1 Peter 5:6** encourage us to approach such errors in judgment—also known as sins?

Fear, when it is justified, is healthy.

Liz Curtis Higgs in *Bad Girls of the Bible*, page 142

7a. Grace and forgiveness seem in short supply in this biblical story. Read **Acts 5:7-10.** Do you think Peter should have told Sapphira what had happened to her husband *before* she was asked the fateful question? Why or why not?

b. Read **Acts 5:8** carefully. What indication do we have that Sapphira may have been given the chance to set the record straight here?

c. What do the following passages further teach us about Sapphira's foolishness?

Isaiah 30:15

Romans 1:20-21

d. Read **Acts 5:5** and **Acts 5:11.** What outcome is recorded in both of these verses?

e. How might such a thing have benefited the early church?

f. What does **Acts 5:14** tell us about the growth of the church *after* this memorable incident?

g. How do you reconcile Sapphira's story of judgment with your understanding of a God who forgives?

h. How might **Ezekiel 18:32** ease your heart?

Honesty isn't the best policy; it's the only policy.

Liz Curtis Higgs in *Bad Girls of the Bible*, page 145

8. What's the most important lesson you've learned from the sad but sinful Sapphira?

KNOCKIN' ON HEAVEN'S DOOR

Rahab

Many women have told me that Rahab is their favorite "Bad Girl"—
and no wonder! Transformed by God from harlot to heroine, this
brave woman is an inspiration for us all, demonstrating how we can leave
behind our shameful pasts and walk forward in grace.

1a. As you read through the story of Rahab in the verses below, under-
line the points below where you most identify with Rahab, then
explain why.
- Her promiscuous past (**Joshua 2:1**)
- Her courageous acts (**Joshua 2:3-6**)
- Her acknowledgment and fear of God (**Joshua 2:8-11**)
- Her concern for family (**Joshua 2:12-13**)
- Her trust in strangers (**Joshua 2:21**)
- Her miraculous redemption (**Joshua 6:22-25**)

b. Former prostitutes are not the only ones among us who need to know that grace and mercy can be found at the throne of God. **Romans 3:22-24** describes our universal need for forgiveness. According to these verses…

where does righteousness come from?

what do we have to do to be forgiven?

how is the grace of God demonstrated?

who needs God's grace and why?

how much does it cost us?

how much did it cost Christ Jesus?

c. Write out **Psalm 86:5.**

Underline all the hope-filled words in that single verse. You may want to memorize this one so you are ready to give a reason for your own hope in Christ.

d. What do the following verses tell us about forgiveness?

Romans 4:7-8

1 John 2:12

e. How can you communicate that forgiveness and hope to the Rahabs among us?

Rahab risked life and limb to hide two men she'd barely met.

Liz Curtis Higgs in *Bad Girls of the Bible*, page 158

2a. Do you ever find yourself unfairly judging women in the church who have a "colorful testimony," avoiding their company or viewing them as distasteful? Think of an example when you've judged someone or felt the sting of judgment yourself.

b. What do the following verses tell us about judging one another?

Luke 6:37

Romans 14:10

James 4:12

c. According to the following verses, how can we push past our preju-
dice—our "prejudgment"—of people and see them simply as sinners
saved by grace, just as we are?

John 13:34-35

Ephesians 4:32

Colossians 3:13-15

1 Peter 3:8

d. In what ways did Rahab demonstrate those virtues?

This wise woman sensed an upheaval...about to sweep through Jericho.   Liz Curtis Higgs in *Bad Girls of the Bible*, page 158

3a. Read **Hebrews 11:31.** Even in the New Testament, Rahab is still known by her old job title. If you identify with Rahab's previous life in some way, what names might you have been called because of your past?

b. If those names still have the power to wound you, the following verses assure us that God has forgiven—and forgotten—those sins and the labels that went with them. Rewrite these verses in the form of a personal praise and thanks from you to God.

Psalm 103:11-12

Psalm 130:3-5

Hebrews 4:15-16

Generous Rahab was even more concerned about the lives of others.   Liz Curtis Higgs in *Bad Girls of the Bible*, page 160

4a. Read **Joshua 2:8-13** again. How many times does Rahab refer to the Lord in these verses?

b. How do we know that Rahab didn't simply tell these men what they wanted to hear so they would spare her life? Are there clues in her behavior that point to true faith—not falsehood—in action?

c. Write out **Romans 10:10.**

Underline the two actions by which we know we are saved.

d. **Joshua 2:11** records Rahab's acknowledgment of the one true God. Find those half dozen words and copy them here.

e. How is Rahab's bold declaration of belief similar to the two simple steps you just underlined from **Romans 10:10**?

> Rahab's sins were as scarlet as the thread that draped from her window.   Liz Curtis Higgs in *Bad Girls of the Bible*, page 161

5a. Read **Joshua 1:2-3; 6:1-5;** and **6:21.** Why did the Lord destroy Jericho and (almost) all of its inhabitants?

b. **Deuteronomy 7:1-5** makes it very clear how such destruction was to be accomplished when the children of Israel entered the Promised Land. Jot down those activities that were indeed carried out in Jericho.

c. According to **Deuteronomy 7:6-10,** why was this claiming of the land necessary?

d. Read **Joshua 2:17-18.** What particular steps of obedience did the spies require of Rahab in order for her to be saved from destruction?

e. Read **Joshua 2:21.** How did she respond verbally?

f. What proof do we have in **Joshua 6:23** that she obeyed physically?

g. In both **Joshua 2:18** and **2:21,** the Hebrew word *tiqvah* is translated as "cord" or "thread." Elsewhere in the Old Testament *tiqvah* is translated as "hope." To what is our *tiqvah*—"hope"—to be tied, according to these passages?

Psalm 71:5-6

1 Timothy 4:9-10

It wasn't Joshua and his army that spared her house—it was God.   Liz Curtis Higgs in *Bad Girls of the Bible*, page 164

6a. One of the themes of this story in Joshua is obedience. Obedience is a choice. List below all the ways various people in this story chose to be obedient…and disobedient.

	OBEDIENT	DISOBEDIENT
Rahab the harlot		
The two Hebrew spies		
The king of Jericho		
Joshua and his soldiers		

b. Read **James 2:25.** What was the result of Rahab's being obedient to God instead of to her heathen king?

c. What do you find in the following verses to motivate you to obedience?

John 14:15

2 John 6

d. Jot down the benefits of obedience as demonstrated in the following two verses.

Romans 16:19

1 John 3:24

e. Read **Joshua 6:25** again and **Matthew 1:1** and **1:5.** What's the happy ending to this Former Bad Girl's story?

f. What does Rahab's new life say to you about God's ability to redeem even the worst among us and to use our lives for his glory?

With God, it isn't who you *were* that matters; it's who you *are* becoming.   Liz Curtis Higgs in *Bad Girls of the Bible*, page 165

7a. Of Rahab's many good qualities, which one impresses you most, and why?

b. Who in your circle of friends demonstrates that same virtue, and how has she done so?

c. How are the truths in **Joshua 24:23-24** a fitting description of Rahab's new life in God?

d. In those verses, Joshua asks two things of the people of God, and they make two promises in return. Write those four statements out here.
(1)

(2)

(3)

(4)

e. Are their "foreign gods" or false idols in your life that need to be thrown away—materialism, a need for control, a self-destructive habit? Rewrite the above four biblical statements as "I will…" promises unto the Lord, praying as you go that you will be as courageous as Rahab was centuries ago and follow through on what you have promised.

"I will

"I will

"I will

"I will

Rahab is remembered not for her harlotry but for her bravery. Not for loving men but for trusting God.

Liz Curtis Higgs in *Bad Girls of the Bible*, page 166

8. What's the most important lesson you've learned from the ultimately redemptive story of Rahab the harlot?

EIGHT

FRIENDS IN LOW PLACES

Jezebel

Oh sure, we love Rahab…but Jezebel? She's another kettle of rotten fish altogether. The problem is some of us identify only too well with pushy Jez, yet another reason we've gotta take a look at her story and learn how to sidestep her unhappy ending.

1a. What descriptive words about Jezebel's personality do these verses bring to mind?

   1 Kings 19:1-2

   1 Kings 21:7-8

   1 Kings 21:15

b. My own list of attributes for Jezebel includes strong-willed, domineering, quick to criticize, eager to take charge, slow to relinquish control, sharp-tongued, stubborn, impatient, and unwilling to admit defeat—all of which could be used to describe *me* on a really bad day! Which one(s) do you identify with most, and why?

c. Through his prophets Isaiah and Jeremiah, the Lord God spoke strongly against the Jezebels of that day *and* this one. What ungodly behaviors did the prophets point to, as recorded in the following verses?

2 Kings 19:22

Isaiah 46:12

Jeremiah 17:23

d. Ahab was equally evil, and it's clear where he learned such behavior. Look what the Bible tells us about his father, King Omri. Jot down the words that point to Omri's wickedness.

1 Kings 16:25

1 Kings 16:26

e. Ahab not only succeeded Omri as king of Israel, he succeeded in topping his dad in the decadence department. According to the following verses, what are some of the things Ahab did that angered God?

1 Kings 16:30

1 Kings 16:31

1 Kings 16:32

1 Kings 16:33

f. Too bad Ahab and Jezebel didn't have **Psalm 40:4** written across the doorpost of their home. Whom does the psalmist say will be blessed...and who will *not* be?

Jezebel's cosmetics couldn't make up for her ugly attitude toward her husband.

Liz Curtis Higgs in *Bad Girls of the Bible*, page 187

2a. An evil man with an evil father married an evil woman with an evil father. No surprise, then, that the marriage was a mess. Reread the fictional exchange between Jasmine and Abe on page 170 in *Bad Girls of the Bible*. What telltale words and actions let us know she didn't respect her husband?

b. Now read the biblical version of that scene in **1 Kings 21:1-7.** Write out Jezebel's dialogue below, one comment or question per line.

1 Kings 21:5

1 Kings 21:5

1 Kings 21:7

1 Kings 21:7

1 Kings 21:7

1 Kings 21:7

c. What tone of voice do you hear in your head while you're reading these verses?

d. Pretend that's *your* man (or teenager!), lying on his bed, sulking and refusing to eat...or go to work...or help with the housework. How might your own commentary sound like Jezebel's words?

e. What do the following verses tell us about how the Lord evaluates our spoken words?

Proverbs 8:13

Matthew 12:34-37

f. **James 3:6** describes how our "tongues" can get us in trouble. If your words—or tone of voice, or attitude—need adjustment, what is the first step you might take toward "cooling down" your speech?

g. Jezebel insisted that *she* would get Ahab his neighbor's vineyard and **1 Kings 21:8-10** tells us how she did it. Ugh. Now turn back to page 56 in *Bad Girls of the Bible.* You'll see in the middle of the page a list of "six things the LORD hates, seven that are detestable to him," all of which Mrs. Potiphar did with gusto. Write those seven things below and note how they also describe Mrs. Ahab's actions. Then comes the hard part: admit to yourself and to God any of those "things" you see in your own life, even in a "softer" form.

SEVEN DETESTABLE THINGS	DONE BY JEZEBEL	DONE BY YOU
(1)		
(2)		
(3)		
(4)		
(5)		
(6)		
(7)		

h. As always, we look to God for his grace and for a way of escape from our sinful inclinations. What does **1 Peter 3:10-11** tell us to do?

i. Maybe you don't identify with pushy Jezebel one tiny bit…but she's a lot like someone you know. Read **Romans 12:16** and **1 Corinthians 13:4-5.** In light of the wisdom found in those verses, how could you lovingly interact with the Jezebels in your life without resorting to their sinful tactics?

When Jezebel spoke, it paid to wear flame-resistant long johns.

Liz Curtis Higgs in *Bad Girls of the Bible*, page 178

3a. For the redeemed Jezebels among us, living the Christian life is a matter of using our God-given natures for his good purposes instead of our bad ones! At the top of page 179 in *Bad Girls of the Bible* you'll find five positive statements about Jezebel. Unfortunately, she used her good qualities for Baal's glory. How could those same attributes be used for God's glory?

ATTRIBUTE	USED FOR GOD'S GLORY
1.	
2.	
3.	
4.	
5.	

b. You *can* be a strong woman and *not* be a Jezebel! Rewrite **1 Corin-thians 16:13** as a checklist of four positive actions for strong believers —your own four "*be* attitudes":

"Be

"Be

"Be

"Be

> The Phoenician princess Jezebel was born rich and in charge.
>
> Liz Curtis Higgs in *Bad Girls of the Bible*, page 177

4a. We learned in **1 Kings 16:31** that Jezebel was the daughter of Eth-baal, whose very name means "man of Baal." Read **1 Kings 22:51-53** and you'll see that Jez and Ahab produced a son equally bent on bending the knee to that false god. If there are children in your immediate circle of influence—family, close friends—whose parents have a highly negative spiritual influence on them, how could you influence those children for righteousness?

b. How might **Matthew 10:42** encourage you to reach out to children who need the "living water" of Christ?

c. For those of us who are parents, **Psalm 34:11** demonstrates our responsibility to our children in spiritual matters. What does it say we are to teach them?

d. Although it might seem more appropriate to teach them the *love* of the Lord or the *grace* of the Lord first, **Proverbs 9:10** explains that wisdom begins with what?

e. What does it mean to *you* to "fear the Lord"?

She didn't offer advice or seek it—she simply took control.

Liz Curtis Higgs in *Bad Girls of the Bible*, page 181

5a. As recorded in **Ezekiel 14:6,** what were the people of Israel commanded to do, in a word?

b. How were they asked to demonstrate their change of heart?

c. Do you think Jezebel was truly "beyond repentance"? Why or why not?

d. The key that unlocks the door to God's grace is repentance. But first we have to realize that we—like Jezebel and everyone else who ever breathed air on this planet other than Jesus himself—are sinners. What do these verses state very clearly?

Isaiah 64:6

Romans 3:9

Romans 3:10

Romans 3:11

Romans 3:12

e. Now the good news! If we repent, God is more than ready to shower us with grace. Written hundreds of years before the birth of Christ, the following verses from the Old Testament attest to the unchangeable nature of a God of forgiveness and mercy. What promises does God make here?

Ezekiel 18:30

Ezekiel 18:31

Ezekiel 18:32

Ezekiel 36:26

Ezekiel 36:27

f. Read **Isaiah 53:6** and **Romans 6:23.** What is God's provision for our sin?

g. Is there an area in your life right now where you need to confess your sin, repent, and accept the sacrificial gift of God's grace?

She was beyond repentance, by her own choice.

Liz Curtis Higgs in *Bad Girls of the Bible*, page 183

6a. We're never told that Jezebel repented; her grisly end, prophesied by Elijah in **1 Kings 21:23-24** is certain proof of that. What about Ahab…did he repent? Read **1 Kings 21:27,** then note several things that Ahab did to demonstrate his change of heart.

b. Read **1 Kings 21:29** to find out how God responded to Ahab's humble display. What "good news" and "bad news" does the Lord pronounce?

Good news:

Bad news:

c. Because Jezebel did not repent, she was not spared. **Proverbs 7:26** might describe Jezebel in her role as the uncrowned queen of Israel. **Proverbs 12:4** might describe Jezebel in her role as the uncrowned queen of Ahab. Why do you think Ahab allowed Jezebel to rule over him?

d. Do you think Ahab contributed to his wife's wicked ways? If so, how?

e. What could Ahab have done to prevent his kingship from turning into the most evil one recorded in Scripture?

Symbolically and literally, the evil queen fell to her death.

Liz Curtis Higgs in *Bad Girls of the Bible*, page 184

7a. The spirit of Jezebel is alive and well in the twenty-first century. Think of a woman you know—public figure or personal acquaintance—who is opposed to your faith or who has her heart set on tearing down Christianity. What would it take to change her attitude toward God?

b. What would it take to change your feelings toward her?

c. For each line of the following verses taken from the Sermon on the
    Plain recorded in Luke, jot down a word or two to remind you what
    a Good Girl needs to do when a modern Jezebel crosses her path.

Luke 6:27

Luke 6:28

Luke 6:29

Luke 6:30

Luke 6:31

Luke 6:36

He gives grace to the humble, but as for the haughty—watch out!   Liz Curtis Higgs in *Bad Girls of the Bible*, page 185

8. What's the most important lesson you've learned from the utterly unlovely story of Ahab and Jezebel?

NINE

OUT OF STEP

Michal

I f you love stories with tragic beginnings and triumphant endings…well, honey, this is not one of 'em. Just the opposite, in fact. A seed of bitterness planted in young Michal's heart bore sour fruit many years later. Yet she provides food for thought for those of us who have a strong-willed father and a "perfect" husband and who feel caught in the forgotten middle.

1a. Everybody loved David. For proof, read **1 Samuel 18:1-7.** According to these verses, who were among his fans?

   1 Samuel 18:1

   1 Samuel 18:5

   1 Samuel 18:6-7

b. If you've ever dated, or been married to, a man who was exceptionally popular or talented, what sort of feelings did that bring out in you?

c. If you've not had that experience, imagine for a moment that you're married to…say, Mel Gibson. Might you feel inadequate? over-whelmed? judged by other women? neglected? jealous of all the atten-tion? or just grateful?! Jot down your thoughts on what life with a celebrity would be like for you.

d. Read **James 3:14-17.** How might you turn any potential jealousy into godly support?

e. Read **Proverbs 14:30.** As we prepare to look at her story in depth, do you think that Michal had a peaceful heart or that she struggled with envy or jealousy?

f. If Michal was the green-eyed type, she had a good teacher—her father. Read **1 Samuel 18:8-9,12.** What emotions are described in those verses?

g. King Saul's jealousy had deep roots, since *he* was once God's chosen and anointed. According to **1 Samuel 16:14,** the Spirit of the Lord had departed from him, and his relationship with God had soured.

Proverbs 27:4 could certainly be applied to Saul's tragic story. Write out the verse from Proverbs here.

h. If you've ever been on the receiving end of someone's jealousy, how did *you* handle it?

i. According to **1 Corinthians 13:4,** what it the best antidote for jealousy—whether we're on the giving *or* receiving end?

> We're told that Michal loved David but never that David loved Michal.   Liz Curtis Higgs in *Bad Girls of the Bible*, page 201

2a. We get to know Michal's father, Saul, quite well. Yet we barely meet her mother, maybe because godly women often don't make the pages of Scripture—that's why the Bad Girls stand out! She is mentioned once, in **1 Samuel 14:49-50,** as the daughter of Ahimaaz and the wife of Saul, along with a listing of their sons and daughters. What is her name?

b. Saul probably made more of a mark on Michal's life if only because of his strong personality. Read **2 Samuel 6:16-23.** List any "like father, like daughter" tendencies Michal demonstrates in that scene.

c. Was your father a positive role model for you or a negative one?

d. What godly things did you learn from him, if any?

e. Are there things your father taught you that you must "unlearn"? If so, what are they and how might you go about doing so?

It wasn't her *altitude* that was the problem. It was her *attitude*.

Liz Curtis Higgs in *Bad Girls of the Bible*, page 207-208

3a. Read **1 Samuel 18:25-27.** How did Saul's plan backfire?

b. Read **1 Samuel 18:28-29.** In these verses, who was on David's side?

c. And who was *not* on David's side?

d. In **1 Samuel 19:11-16** you'll find Michal proving her love for David by helping him avoid her father's henchmen. Jot down a word or two from each verse that describes the *action* she took and the *attitude* that might have motivated her behavior. For example:

	ACTION	POSITIVE ATTITUDE
1 Samuel 19:11	*warned David*	*genuine concern*
1 Samuel 19:12		
1 Samuel 19:13		
1 Samuel 19:14		

e. This is the heroic side of Michal's character. What is there about Michal that you wish you could emulate—her courage, her cleverness, her creativity?

f. When we meet Michal years later, her actions and attitude have soured. How can we avoid going "sour" as we age?

[David] remembered the price but not the princess all those years.   Liz Curtis Higgs in *Bad Girls of the Bible*, page 206

4a. Michal was bitter about being ignored by David for fourteen years, but she *did* help him run away in the first place. Read **1 Samuel 19:17** and consider the dilemma this daughter *and* wife faced when her father found out about David's escape. Whom does Saul blame...and why?

b. Whom does Michal blame...and why?

c. Would David really have killed her? Why or why not?

d. What might it have cost Michal to blame the true culprit, her father?

e. What does **Deuteronomy 5:16** command a son or daughter to do?

f. What does **Genesis 2:24** command a man or wife to do?

g. To whom was Michal's first allegiance—her husband or her father?

h. How might **Ephesians 5:22** answer that question?

i. **Psalm 59:1-5** gives us David's version of the same scene. According to verse 5, whom does David blame?

j. And whom does David call on for help?

k. How might the Lord have used Michal's bravery for his good purpose?

When it came to godly obedience, Michal was off the mark.

Liz Curtis Higgs in *Bad Girls of the Bible*, page 208

5a. Things took a turn for the worse for Michal. Read **1 Samuel 25:44.** Do you think Saul was punishing Michal…or punishing David? Why?

b. According to **Deuteronomy 22:22,** what did Mosaic Law have to say about the situation with Michal and Paltiel?

c. How might Saul, who knew Mosaic Law, have convinced himself he had a right to do this?

d. Perhaps King Saul was so convinced David was as good as dead, he proclaimed him so. What does **1 Corinthians 7:39** tell us in a case such as that?

e. Why do you think Paltiel agreed to take this married woman?

f. How does the New Testament address a wife's responsibilities when her husband is not with her? Read **1 Corinthians 7:10-11.**

g. Are both parties held accountable or only one?

h. Apparently Michal had no choice in the matter. How might a godly woman have managed to honor her marriage vows, even when her father didn't? Consider the following choices, then note the possible ramifications of those options.

OPTION   **RAMIFICATION**

Run away and find David

Refuse to go with Paltiel

Enlist Paltiel's help in finding David

She...determined to be miserable forever. And so she was.

Liz Curtis Higgs in *Bad Girls of the Bible*, page 210

6a. Forced to live apart from the man she loved and forced to live with a man that she did not choose, Michal's young heart must have been sorely broken. If you've ever been forced into a situation you *knew* was wrong, how did you handle it?

b. If it happened when you were younger, how would you handle it today?

c. How might **2 Corinthians 4:16-17** give you the strength to endure a difficult situation?

d. Read **Psalm 56:4**, then answer the question the psalmist raises.

e. How does that verse encourage you?

f. **First Peter 3:13-14** also poses a question. How might you answer it?

g. How is it possible to feel blessed when we suffer?

h. **Ecclesiastes 7:14** delivers a pretty tough message. What, in a nut-shell, does it say?

i. And what does it say to *you*, in your life right now?

David's dancing didn't turn her heart; it turned her stomach.

Liz Curtis Higgs in *Bad Girls of the Bible*, page 208

7a. At last, David and Michal met again. Read **2 Samuel 3:12-14.** What does David demand of Abner, Saul's son?

b. In verse 14, David reminds Abner of what important fact?

c. Note an interesting statement made about David in **2 Samuel 3:36.**
   What does that tell you about David's people skills?

d. Considering the evidence we're given in Scripture, do you think
   David loved his wife Michal? Why or why not?

e. How did David's love for Michal (or lack of it) affect her responsibility to honor God?

f. Read **Isaiah 54:5.** Ultimately, who could have served as husband to
   Michal all those years?

g. How might that verse comfort you—married, single, divorced, or
   widowed?

h. Read page 209 of *Bad Girls of the Bible*. What are the three problems I thought Michal might have found in David's dance?

(1)

(2)

(3)

i. What do I suggest David saw in Michal's eyes?

j. Now open your Bible to this climactic scene—**2 Samuel 6:14-22**— and read it straight through. What is your impression of David's actions here?

k. And how does Michal's response strike you?

l. Who did David put first in his life…himself, Michal, or God?

m. How does **2 Samuel 6:23** sum up the rest of Michal's life?

n. Why was this the worst possible news for her?

o. How does the thought of such a thing impact *you?*

p. Now read **Acts 13:22-23.** What does it mean that David was "a man after God's own heart?"

q. Who would be the long-awaited descendant of David?

r. Why could Michal not be part of that family lineage?

Bad Girls blame their situations. Good Girls rise above them.

Liz Curtis Higgs in *Bad Girls of the Bible*, page 212

---

8. What's the most important lesson you learned from the story of Michal, a woman ultimately *not* seeking after God's own heart or her husband's either?

TEN

I BEG YOUR PARDON

The Sinful Woman

Keep a box of tissues handy. There's something about this nameless sister's story and her total abandonment of self at the feet of her Savior that goes straight to our hearts...and to our tear ducts. Don't be embarrassed, beloved. It's those very tears that help us identify with her sorrowful repentance *and* her joyful freedom in Christ.

1a. Read **Luke 7:37.** Based on that verse alone, what do we know about this woman?

b. And what *don't* we know about this woman?

c. In the fictional introduction to this chapter, I gave this woman the name *Anita* because she was drawn to this party by *a need to* demonstrate her love and gratitude to this holy, grace-filled man. Let's see how she did that. All the scandalous steps are gathered into one verse: **Luke 7:38.** Where was she standing and why?

d. Why wasn't she lurking around the corners of the room with the other uninvited guests?

e. Specifically, what does she do to the feet of Jesus?

First she…

Then she…

Next she…

Finally she…

f. Now read the fictional scene from the bottom of page 218 to the top of 219 in *Bad Girls of the Bible*. What brought Anita to tears?

g. What phrases, if any, touch *you* emotionally?

h. Note any symbolic language in this passage that points to Jesus.

i. Think of an occasion when you were overwhelmed, unable to speak, and found yourself weeping instead. How did that make you feel? Weak? Embarrassed? Relieved? Cleansed?

j. Let's see how the sinful woman might have felt. Read page 224 of *Bad Girls of the Bible,* where I suggested several emotions that probably started her tears flowing. Jot them down here from the text.

k. Now add any that I might have missed, and underline the one or two that best express your own heart.

l. Read **Joel 2:12-13.** What was the Lord asking his people to do?

m. What expressions of repentance did he expect to see from them?

n. What reception are they told to anticipate?

o. How might those verses from Joel parallel what we see at work in this weeping woman's life?

What would a woman of the street want with a man of the
cloth?   Liz Curtis Higgs in *Bad Girls of the Bible*, page 222

2a. Read **Luke 7:38** again. What motivates people to break the bonds of convention and "let down their hair" in seeking to worship the Lord?

b. Look up these biblical examples of variety and creativity in worship, and jot down the expressive activity in each one.

1 Chronicles 29:20

Psalm 47:5

Psalm 95:6

Psalm 149:3

Psalm 150:5

c. In which of these forms of worship have you been a participant?

d. What other means of corporate worship have you experienced?

e. What was the result of those activities…applause for man or applause for God?

f. Read **Psalm 19:14** and **Romans 12:1.** How do we know if our worship is pleasing to God?

g. If you would, stand up and read **1 Chronicles 16:23-36** out loud. Yes, all of it! Alone at home or together in your study group, worship the Lord simply by reading his Holy Word out loud with all the honor and majesty it deserves. When you sit down, write the first thought that comes to mind.

Alabaster jars were common—it was the substance hidden inside that was valuable.   Liz Curtis Higgs in *Bad Girls of the Bible*, page 223

3a. Foot kissing and perfume pouring might not be on your to-do list for next Sunday morning's worship service. But what could you do—privately or publicly—that would be as sacrificial and meaningful as this woman's actions?

b. Would you be willing to try it? In public or private?

c. How might you do it, practically speaking?

d. What would be the benefit, spiritually speaking?

e. Worship is different than listening to a sermon or studying the Bible or singing hymns, although those elements may be part of a worship service. Above all things, we're called to seek the face of God. What words in the following verses speak to your heart's need for worship?

1 Chronicles 16:10-11

Psalm 5:7

Psalm 27:4

f. **First Peter 5:14** tells us how the early church members greeted one another. But this woman takes that practice to a whole new, outrageous level. How much would you have to love someone to kiss his or her adult feet?

g. What possessed our nameless worshiper to do such a thing?

h. Read **Luke 7:39.** What attitudes do Simon's thoughts convey concerning the woman at Jesus' feet?

i. Was that perfume appealing to him, do you think...or disgusting?

j. The apostle Paul wrote that we who love God bear the fragrant aroma of Christ. Read the last sentence of the fictional account on page 221 of *Bad Girls of the Bible,* and write down any descriptive words for the perfume you find there.

k. That is how the world around us perceives our unavoidable "fragrance." According to **2 Corinthians 2:14-16,** what exactly is that fragrance?

l. Who finds that scent appealing?

m. And who thinks it stinks?

n. Do we have any means of controlling people's reaction to our spiritual "scent"?

His utter sinlessness undid her.

Liz Curtis Higgs in *Bad Girls of the Bible*, page 224

4a. It was time for Simon the Pharisee to learn a lesson. Read **Luke 7:40-43.** Write out the question that Jesus asked him.

b. What do you think Jesus was really asking him?

c. In **Luke 7:44-46,** Jesus pointed out the things Simon *didn't* do and the things she *did* do. Compare their activities here, as described in each verse.

	THE PHARISEE...	THE SINFUL WOMAN...
Verse 44		
Verse 45		
Verse 46		

d. What one thing do you observe that Simon the Pharisee *did* do that the woman never does in this scene?

e. What does her silence convey to you?

f. Read **Job 6:24.** How might that verse suit this scene?

g. Do you identify more with the chatty woman at the well or this silent sinner at Jesus' feet?

His grace only increased her devotion.

Liz Curtis Higgs in *Bad Girls of the Bible*, page 224

5a. **Luke 7:47** is a much-quoted verse of Scripture…at least the first half! At the start of the story she is called a "sinful woman." Is there any doubt that she was completely forgiven by story's end? What makes you confident of your answer?

b. In **Luke 7:48** we see that Jesus was no longer speaking to the Pharisee. Who, then?

c. He has already stated this to Simon. Why does he repeat it?

d. How can we know, as surely as this woman did, that our sins are forgiven? Read the following verses and write out the key phrases that most speak to you, rephrasing them in first person—"so great is his love for *me*," etc.

Psalm 103:11-12

Romans 4:7

Romans 5:8

Ephesians 1:7-8

1 John 2:12

Standing so close to him, she knew—knew!—that Jesus alone
understood her, forgave her, loved her.

Liz Curtis Higgs in *Bad Girls of the Bible*, page 224

6a. Good news like that makes me want to shout his grace from the
rooftops! What do you imagine this quiet, humble woman did to
spread the good news?

b. Sometimes the hardest people to share the gospel with are our own
family members. What does **1 Peter 3:1-2** suggest instead of telling
them with words?

c. In **Ephesians 4:2** we find a simple list of attributes that speak louder
than words. What are they?

d. At the bottom of page 232 of *Bad Girls of the Bible* you'll find four
steps this Former Bad Girl took—and we can take as well—to know
the fullness of God's mercy. List them below, noting on a scale of 1 to
5 how difficult each one is for you to do, with 1 being "easy" and 5
being "very hard." Take a moment to think through how you might
turn your 4s and 5s into 1s.

WHAT TO DO	DEGREE OF DIFFICULTY FOR YOU				
(1)	1	2	3	4	5
(2)	1	2	3	4	5
(3)	1	2	3	4	5
(4)	1	2	3	4	5

She not only broke open her jar, she shattered the mold of
how worship was to be done.

Liz Curtis Higgs in *Bad Girls of the Bible*, page 230

7a. Simon the Pharisee wasn't the only person who heard Jesus extend
forgiveness to the sinful woman. Read **Luke 7:49.** Did they seem to
be impressed…or incensed?

b. When people watch someone turn from an openly sinful life to an openly grace-filled one, they are naturally curious, if not cautious or even downright cynical. The book of Acts records the story of Saul (who would soon be Paul) and his conversion. Neither the Jews nor the Christians trusted his testimony! Read **Acts 9:26-28.** Who or what did it take for the young church to be convinced Saul's conversion was genuine?

c. Whatever our testimony might be, how can we convince folks we're a "new creation"?

d. To what extent is a Former Bad Girl responsible for proving her new status?

e. Read **Jude 22-23.** How are we to respond to those who doubt our faith?

f. Read **Luke 7:50,** the last verse in our story. According to Jesus, what has saved this woman?

g. Jesus sent her off with what benediction?

h. How might **Psalm 85:8** sum up the attitude of this woman's heart?

i. Do you think this woman went back to her old life? Why or why not?

Love and gratitude filled the air with the fragrant aroma of a soul set free.   Liz Curtis Higgs in *Bad Girls of the Bible*, page 233

8. What's the most important lesson you learned from the story of this sinful-but-forgiven woman?

A Last Word from Liz

You did it! I'm proud of you, girlfriend.

I hope this workbook not only guided you through the pages of Scripture but also illuminated some of the darker corners of your heart. That's what happens when we get to know Jesus. "I am the light of the world. Whoever follows me will never walk in darkness, but will have the light of life" (John 8:12).

Shine on, sis.

As with all projects, this one didn't happen alone. My dear sister in speaking and in Christ, Glenna Salsbury, provided several dynamite questions to enhance these pages. Another Bible study pro, Lynn Reece, gave me valued feedback in the important early stages. Rebecca Price served as chief cheerleader; Laura Barker, Carol Bartley, and Stephanie Terry offered gentle editorial guidance; and my dear hubby, Bill, did what he does best: endlessly encourage me even while wielding a sharp red pencil.

If you're ready to tackle *Really Bad Girls of the Bible,* you'll find the best-selling book, workbook, and video waiting at a bookstore near you, as well as my third book in the Bad Girls collection, *Unveiling Mary Magdalene.* What a blessing it would be to open God's Word with you again!

Even with fourteen hundred speaking engagements behind me and eighteen published books, I still have so *much* to learn. My readers are an important part of that growing process, and I'm honored and grateful when readers take time to drop me a line by post or e-mail:

Liz@LizCurtisHiggs.com

Liz Curtis Higgs

P.O. Box 43577

Louisville, KY 40253-0577

Until our paths cross again, dear one, may you grow in grace!